FOOTSTEPS

DOORS

Included

S. E. McKenzie

DEDICATION
To everyone who has been left out in the cold

This book is a book of speculative fiction.
Characters, companies, governments, places, events, are either products of the author's imagination or used fictitiously. Any resemblance to persons (living or dead), companies, governments, places and/or events, is a coincidence.

TABLE OF CONTENTS

FOOTSTEPS

FOOTSTEPS

I

As a boy
David walked beside his shadow
For his body was soaking up light

Which surrounded him.
He learned to gentlefy his might,
While showing Love to everything in sight.

He avoided every battle and every fight.
His shadow was invisible,
When there was little light.

He stood behind the tree
As Goliath showed his might
His weapon of war was to offend

Never making a friend; so willing to exclude.
Dehumanization; Group-think so rude.
As isolation drove the enemy mad,

Goliath knew how to be bad.
Fraternization was never allowed
That was how he controlled the crowd.

S.E. McKENZIE

Life was better for the in-crowd
And everyone agreed
Except Saul

There were problems and hard times
Behind his wall
Because Saul didn't want to fall

There was mistrust
And fear of occupation
There was a thirst for a new sensation

And David cried out in pain
Let me go
So I may know

My higher power
Will guide me
To be the best I can be

Let my feet take me down the path
And during the night
The light will show me the way

FOOTSTEPS: Doors Included

I need divine rights of man
So my spirit can pulsate freely
Regardless of the rewriting of history

I want to grow my mind
I want to be always kind
Never willfully blind

In the future years
Driven by my Momma's tears
I shall free myself from all my Fears."

And Goliath roared from behind
"Everyone is so small
Compared to me

I am a magnet for riches and glory
While I strangle you in poverty
And war so gory

For my footsteps
Create my path
And I will leave you in my aftermath

As I bring ruin to those behind that wall
I demand to see Saul
So I may watch him fall.

As a force of nature
I shall seal your fate."
And David replied,

"And without Love,
Thou shall be poisoned by your hate,
That is how you will seal your fate.

My strength dear King,
Will show in the ring,
As I throw my five stones,

My footsteps too will create my path,
And I too will live in your aftermath,
And you will be the one to take the bath.

I shall unlock the gate of fate on this site
While His light in the night
Will show me the way."

FOOTSTEPS: Doors Included

II

"The path is mine
Cause I push and shove
You play your harp and speak of Love,

How do you expect to win?"
"I will win because His light shines upon my path
My footsteps are gentle and meek

Your roar is hard to ignore
And when you fall
The earth around you might crumble

But no one will grumble
For the Fear you spread
Will soon be dead."

"I foresee you under my feet
If you don't step aside
And find a place to hide

Let your king fight me."
"No, I hear the call."
"You must, I want Saul."

"No, you can't have it all
Just because you are tall
And I am small

I will go beyond my station
His light upon my path
Will lead me to my destination.

My feet shall follow this path
For I know how to bend when I see HIs light
And that is how I will mend

Whatever you may break
Will never hide your weakness
Letting it show, will be your last mistake."

III
Oh free spirit
How you roam
Do you ever crave a home?

You are free of obligation
Except to life
You have no restraint

FOOTSTEPS: Doors Included

You tear down walls
That get in the way
For freedom builds your might.

As the tyrant screamed out in rage
"You threaten my authority
And you do it in every page."

"Time brings life and time brings death
Time brought you your very first breath.
Time is forever but not for you."

As the free spirit grew deep in him
He was so afraid to be confined
By the cruel mastermind

Could not be defined
By the tyrant as he screamed
Watch the slaves awake

From their broken dreams
For they know the cost
Of never being free

For they are chained to the tyrant's misery.
Rewrite history
If you must.

As the tyrant pushed and shoved
David wrote poems
Of Peace and Love.

IV
Excitement of war is in the air
The tyrant wants that land
Over there

The soldiers will die in despair
But the tyrant won't ever care
He must have that land over there

The trumpets blare for the war has begun
And some will awake to the new day in the sun
Wondering if the peace will ever be won

Listen to the bell, for it will ring
Misinformation is in the spring
Close the freeways and all the ports

FOOTSTEPS: Doors Included

We will bunk together, in our humble forts.

See the divided world, it hoped for peace,
The way jilted lovers hoped for Love,
But peace was just a dream on this field of war

Drums of war electrify the heart
They summon feet to march in time
Before the enemy is torn apart

Down the street and around the bend
Once in war
It is hard to mend.

"Close your eyes and forget the past"
The king said very fast.
He sat on his throne

As commerce stood still
Able men were gone
Lost in struggle, goodwill was still feared.

No one wanted to be conquered
And were willing to die instead
The Fear could not stop, it was lost in their head.

S.E. McKENZIE

As hostilities took heart
No one wanted to die
Time moved forward and could not go back

The manufactured hatred
Let the tyrant take control
"We must gain and maintain our dominant role"

We must prevent chaos
We are the boss and they are not
Let nature take them over and let them rot."

"Bury the plowshares
Never share the food
Let the enemy's hunger force him to brood"

The King said
As he sat on his throne
"Make the enemy feel isolated and all alone

Make him feel glum
So he will drown
In his own rum."

FOOTSTEPS: Doors Included

The soldiers wanted peace
And wanted to go home
They did not want war or to be forced to roam

Upon a scorched Earth
Trapped in no man's land
The soldiers wanted a peaceful plan

But were trapped
On land
No longer fit for man

For he knew no other way
To maintain
The free spirit that he was

So afraid to be confined
By the mastermind
He refused to be defined

By the willfully blind
Who should have known
The cost

Of never being free
He must step softly
Around this giant adversary

That opposes and attacks
That defames behind backs
Toxic vulture culture

Was all around
"You must try to stand your ground
If you can."

In a place where they love to ban
Anyone they can
Just for the thrill

The stress made their adversaries ill.

Toxic commodification
No concern for what was lost
Condescending and never ending

Made the steely tyrant
Feel in control
Like a chain gang boss

FOOTSTEPS: Doors Included

You must tread lightly
Around all this chaos
For Living Light will shine upon your ground

For silence is his power
So don't utter a sound
If you want to stick around

In this pump and dump town.

V

Free spirits roamed
On the earth before it was scorched and worn
Pages were written then torn

Praising the Earth's beauty
When nature was free and not just worn
Now nature is property

And lost peace
Raged as war.
What was lost

Was priceless
And no one would know
The cost

The trees were cut down
The waters turned brown
The ice began to melt

And so did the snow
The wild creatures
Had very few places to go.

The wild creatures
Were part of His Plan
Even the ones dependent on man.

One had to believe in the Golden Age
And then step aside
So that the green could be seen.

THE END

DOORS

DOORS

I

World War I wasn't fun
World War II well it made you
World War III is all around Lee

For Lee is a victim
Of what
He can't see.

Lee can't hear the roar of war
Though he has felt war
Many times before.

Lee gets up from his floor
And rushes through his door.
Making sure his hope

Stays intact
For bad vibes from spoken words
Are weapons of choice

In a world where domination
Of the despicables
Gain power from the reflections they see

FOOTSTEPS: Doors Included

Making it so easy to persecute Lee.

For reversing a broken heart
Is easier said than done
Overwhelmed by Dark Days hidden by the sun

Lee would feel despair,
In a world of strangers
Who pretend to care.

Fog is in the air
Droplets of water all around
Not yet soaking into the ground

War is destruction's rope
To win one must be
Never numbed with fear

And Peace is more
Than just the absence of War
This has been said many times before.

Peace cannot be commodified
Though is often buried
In words that have lied.

Just like Love;
Recharges
Everyday

Electrifying and never in the way

Nature's Electricity
Creates light
Helps Lee see

Into the night

Sometimes Lee thinks
There is too much light
Until the fog comes rolling through

Mariana said,
"No need to shout
I am on Facebook deleting my friend out."

Lee knew someone had lied

Lee replied,
"I feel so much doubt
I feel there is no way out."

FOOTSTEPS: Doors Included

Lee and Mariana
Held hands real tight
As they watched the low clouds

Flow through the night

II

And the years went by
Mariana spent half her life
Deleting her friends on Facebook

For they all had lied
While she cried
Even though Facebook filled

Her emptiness inside.

And all through life
Lee faced doors;
Doors that could only be walked through

One door at a time.
Some would open
And some would close

Many doors could never be opened again.

Lee soon learned the secret of serenity
He found the key
To the only door needed

The door led to a room of his own

In a world
As cold as stone
Many would never have a room to call their own.

As the years went by
Many doors closed in Lee's face
It was such a sad state

Feelings of disgrace.
Were replaced with hate
Only negative emotions were shared so freely

For fighting for Love
Was so out of date
So many preferred this feeling of hate

Faces were captured all around
Some so sad
They chose to be buried in the ground

FOOTSTEPS: Doors Included

How could his life begin
When no one would open the door
To let Lee in?

Lee continued to follow his path.

And the years went by
And many pages were turned
Many called the journey's path life

Even though many never opened the door
To the room in their mind
Their lost life was the aftermath

And their anger made them unkind
They were so trapped in feelings
Of gloom and doom.

Closed doors slammed in Lee's face
Were soon forgot
Only Fear could paralyze; leaving his mind to rot.

How could Lee be free?
No longer in charge of his destiny
Inside his mind there was no room

No shelter from his pain and gloom.
So how could his true love bloom?
Love was now outdated and doomed to a tomb.

Lee turned away
The war was raging and out of sight
There were no winners

Even though both sides
Fought with all their might
All through the night

Peace could not be created
Between people
Who were trapped in hatred

And despair
How could Lee know true Love
When Marianna was never there

She was on Facebook
Deleting friends
Who had stabbed her in the back

FOOTSTEPS: Doors Included

Due to the loss
Each one felt
When they found refuge

Behind locked doors.

III

Once there was a mountain
Too high to climb
Until the ladders were built

And guides were willing
To show the way.
Once climbed

One could see the beauty all around
Above from the fog not yet soaked
Into the ground

The world was in danger
For the tyrant was ruling
With an iron fist

And narrow scope of vision
Made it an easier decision
To offend a stranger than befriend

Easier to hate the foreign
Confined affairs of others
By new legalistic rules written by fools.

And the evil grew.
So many lied and said
That it was not true.

When the evil grows out of control
The evil could grow
Stronger than you

So shut the door
Like you have done many times before
And don't be afraid any more

See the world
On the other side
Of this window pane

Not yet broken by torrential winds
And do you see who must hide
And who is thrown away

And who gets the final say?

FOOTSTEPS: Doors Included

IV

Lee and Mariana
Let time slip by
Grew a family

And as they grew
Each had a door
To their room

Which shielded them
As the years went by
More flags waved in the air

More graves were dug
Brave soldiers
Were drinking the legal drug in a jug

As time went by
Many would die
The ones left could no longer cry

The death of Hope
Was never mourned
And the dictatorship of Fear

Was followed and never scorned.
"Don't walk through that door,"
Mariana warned

"Without a goal
You will forever stroll
Under the control

Of that dictator troll."

"Thank you for warning me," said Lee.
"Don't wanna be perturbed and hated
Don't wanna live behind that door

For evermore.
Our life is the way it needs to be
For me to stay true to you

Our Love sets us on fire
And has freed us
From their power of Fear

And that power of Fear
Holds them all night
In a state of fright.

FOOTSTEPS: Doors Included

How can they love
When what they fear
Is so anticipated?

Don't wanna be
Trapped behind that door
While their force feeds their bias so strong

Keeps them all so captivated
Without seeing the wrong
So tangled up in their war

Of words designed to fit
The late night culture
Ancient confirmation bias

Which was said to have trapped
The Dictator Troll's mind
A long time ago

And made him blind
To what could have been
Within a future

Not yet seen
And still an empty chance of fate
Free from any bias of hate

The future shall not be sealed
The ruler said from his throne in a make believe Camelot
"Dreams cannot die and never be shot.

They tell you to fear anger
But Fear can make you rot
Paralyzed so afraid of being shot.

V

Walking through the revolving door
Done so many times before
Ghosts hidden in shadows

Went in and out for the ride
They were all dead
No need now for false pride.

Dead birds at your door step
Were thrown down the hall
For no reason at all.

FOOTSTEPS: Doors Included

In hope and anticipation
It was true
That tear drops blurred your eyes

Dark clouds over your head
Negative words
Create so much dread

Marianna's friends
Were not dead
Just deleted instead

Fear blinded the eyes
Too painful to see
Insight to future opportunity

As the dead were the very few
Who could still feel free."
Said Lee.

Lee opened the door
And saw the sun
He wondered what had been done

Negative words
Weapon of choice
Hopelessness numbed the mind

Love was worth fighting for
Love was kind
And no one would disagree

Trust could build Goodwill

But if not
One could rot
Under the battlefield

For evermore

World War I wasn't fun
World War II well it made you
World War III is all around Lee

For Lee is a victim
Of what
He can't see.

THE END

Produced by S.E. McKenzie Productions
First Print Edition April 2015

Enquiries: 1(778)992-2453
Mailing Address:
S. E. McKenzie Productions
168 B 5th St.
Courtenay, BC
V9N 1J4

Email Address:
messidartha@aol.com

http://www.amazon.com/SarahMcKenzie/e/B00H9RWX48/ref=ntt
_dp_epwbk_0

www.ingramcontent.com/pod-product-compliance
Lightning Source LLC
Chambersburg PA
CBHW060546030426
42337CB00021B/4453